the
FEMINIST
agenda

UNIVERSE

Published by UNIVERSE PUBLISHING

A Division of Rizzoli International Publications, Inc.

300 Park Avenue South

New York, NY 10010

www.rizzoliusa.com

Design by Celina Carvalho

Printed in Hong Kong, PRC

One is not born, but rather becomes, a woman.

SIMONE DE BEAUVOIR

.... , 20 ....

MON

....

TUE

....

WED

....

THU

....

FRI

....

SAT

....

SUN

....

I hate to hear you talk about all women as if they were fine ladies instead of rational creatures. None of us want to be in calm waters all our lives.

JANE AUSTEN

I raise up my voice—not so I can shout, but so that those without a voice can be heard. . . . We cannot all succeed when half of us are held back.

MALALA YOUSAFZAI

.... , 20........

MON

....

TUE

....

WED

....

THU

....

FRI

....

SAT

....

SUN

....

.... , 20........

MON
....

TUE
....

WED
....

THU
....

FRI
....

SAT
....

SUN
....

Figure out who you are separate from your family, and the man or woman you're in a relationship with. Find who you are in this world and what you need to feel good alone. I think that's the most important thing in life. Find a sense of self because, with that, you can do anything else.

ANGELINA JOLIE

Women must try to do things as
men have tried. When they fail,
their failure must be but a challenge
to others.

AMELIA EARHART

.... , 20 ....

MON

....

TUE

....

WED

....

THU

....

FRI

....

SAT

....

SUN

....

.... , 20........

MON

....

TUE

....

WED

....

THU

....

FRI

....

SAT

....

SUN

....

Feminism is not here to dictate to you. It's not prescriptive, it's not dogmatic. All we are here to do is give you a choice.

EMMA WATSON

No person is your friend who demands your silence, or denies your right to grow.

ALICE WALKER

.... , 20.........

MON

....

TUE

....

WED

....

THU

....

FRI

....

SAT

....

SUN

....

.... , 20........

MON

....

TUE

....

WED

....

THU

....

FRI

....

SAT

....

SUN

....

Women belong in all places
where decisions are being made. . . .
It shouldn't be that women are
the exception.

RUTH BADER GINSBURG

We come in peace, but we mean business. And to those who would dare try and silence us, we offer you two words: Time's Up.

JANELLE MONÁE

.... , 20........

MON

....

TUE

....

WED

....

THU

....

FRI

....

SAT

....

SUN

....

.... , 20........

MON

....

TUE

....

WED

....

THU

....

FRI

....

SAT

....

SUN

....

No one can make you feel inferior
without your consent.

ELEANOR ROOSEVELT

We're held to a different standard than men. Some guy said to me: "Don't you think you're too old to sing rock and roll?" I said: "You'd better check with Mick Jagger."

CHER

.... , 20 ....

MON

....

TUE

....

WED

....

THU

....

FRI

....

SAT

....

SUN

....

.... , 20.........

MON

....

TUE

....

WED

....

THU

....

FRI

....

SAT

....

SUN

....

The most courageous act is still
to think for yourself. Aloud.

COCO CHANEL

Each person must live their life
as a model for others.

ROSA PARKS

.... , 20.........

MON

....

TUE

....

WED

....

THU

....

FRI

....

SAT

....

SUN

....

.... , 20........

MON

....

TUE

....

WED

....

THU

....

FRI

....

SAT

....

SUN

....

Despite all the challenges we
face, I remain convinced that yes,
the future is female.

HILLARY CLINTON

Find something you're passionate
about and keep tremendously
interested in it.

JULIA CHILD

.... , 20.........

MON

....

TUE

....

WED

....

THU

....

FRI

....

SAT

....

SUN

....

.... , 20 ....

MON

....

TUE

....

WED

....

THU

....

FRI

....

SAT

....

SUN

....

We do not need magic to transform
our world. We carry all the power
we need inside ourselves already; we
have the power to imagine better.

J.K. ROWLING

You can be the lead in
your own life.

KERRY WASHINGTON

.... , 20 ....

MON

....

TUE

....

WED

....

THU

....

FRI

....

SAT

....

SUN

....

.... , 20 ....

MON

....

TUE

....

WED

....

THU

....

FRI

....

SAT

....

SUN

....

Alone we can do so little;
together we can do so much.

HELEN KELLER

My point is, life is about balance.
The good and the bad. The
highs and the lows. The piña
and the colada.

ELLEN DEGENERES

.... , 20........

MON

....

TUE

....

WED

....

THU

....

FRI

....

SAT

....

SUN

....

.... , 20 ....

MON

....

TUE

....

WED

....

THU

....

FRI

....

SAT

....

SUN

....

I'm no longer accepting the things
I cannot change. I'm changing the
things I cannot accept.

ANGELA DAVIS

A feminist is anyone who recognizes
the equality and full humanity of
women and men.

GLORIA STEINEM

.... , 20.........

MON

....

TUE

....

WED

....

THU

....

FRI

....

SAT

....

SUN

....

.... , 20 ....

MON

....

TUE

....

WED

....

THU

....

FRI

....

SAT

....

SUN

....

The success of every woman should be the inspiration to another. We should raise each other up. Make sure you're very courageous: be strong, be extremely kind, and above all, be humble.

SERENA WILLIAMS

Of course I am not worried about intimidating men. The type of man who will be intimidated by me is exactly the type of man I have no interest in.

CHIMAMANDA NGOZI ADICHIE

.... , 20 ....

MON

....

TUE

....

WED

....

THU

....

FRI

....

SAT

....

SUN

....

.... , 20.........

MON

....

TUE

....

WED

....

THU

....

FRI

....

SAT

....

SUN

....

I finally got my answer to that question: Who do you think you are? I am whoever I say I am.

AMERICA FERRERA

My hope for the future, not just in the music industry, but in every young girl I meet, is that they all realize their worth and ask for it.

TAYLOR SWIFT

.... , 20.........

MON

....

TUE

....

WED

....

THU

....

FRI

....

SAT

....

SUN

....

.... , 20.........

MON

....

TUE

....

WED

....

THU

....

FRI

....

SAT

....

SUN

....

There's many women now who think, "Surely we don't need feminism anymore, we're all liberated and society's accepting us as we are." Which is all just hogwash. It's not true at all.

YOKO ONO

Some women choose to follow men, and some women choose to follow their dreams. If you're wondering which way to go, remember that your career will never wake up and tell you that it doesn't love you anymore.

LADY GAGA

.... , 20 ....

MON

....

TUE

....

WED

....

THU

....

FRI

....

SAT

....

SUN

....

.... , 20 ....

MON

....

TUE

....

WED

....

THU

....

FRI

....

SAT

....

SUN

....

I will not have my life narrowed
down. I will not bow down to
somebody else's whim or to
someone else's ignorance.

BELL HOOKS

I'd rather regret the things I've done than regret the things I haven't done.

LUCILLE BALL

.... , 20........

MON

....

TUE

....

WED

....

THU

....

FRI

....

SAT

....

SUN

....

.... , 20.........

MON

....

TUE

....

WED

....

THU

....

FRI

....

SAT

....

SUN

....

Think like a queen. A queen is
not afraid to fail. Failure is another
stepping-stone to greatness.

OPRAH WINFREY

I say if I'm beautiful. I say if I'm
strong. You will not determine
my story—I will.

AMY SCHUMER

.... , 20........

MON

....

TUE

....

WED

....

THU

....

FRI

....

SAT

....

SUN

....

.... , 20.........

MON

....

TUE

....

WED

....

THU

....

FRI

....

SAT

....

SUN

....

We need to reshape our own
perception of how we view
ourselves. We have to step up as
women and take the lead.

BEYONCÉ

Abandon the cultural myth that all female friendships must be bitchy, toxic, or competitive. This myth is like heels and purses—pretty but designed to SLOW women down.

ROXANE GAY

.... , 20........

MON

....

TUE

....

WED

....

THU

....

FRI

....

SAT

....

SUN

....

.... , 20........

MON

....

TUE

....

WED

....

THU

....

FRI

....

SAT

....

SUN

....

I just love bossy women. I could be around them all day. To me, bossy is not a pejorative term at all. It means somebody's passionate and engaged and ambitious and doesn't mind leading.

AMY POEHLER

When I'm hungry, I eat. When I'm
thirsty, I drink. When I feel like
saying something, I say it.

MADONNA

.... , 20.........

MON

....

TUE

....

WED

....

THU

....

FRI

....

SAT

....

SUN

....

.... , 20........

MON

....

TUE

....

WED

....

THU

....

FRI

....

SAT

....

SUN

....

You may not control all the events
that happen to you, but you can
decide not to be reduced by them.

MAYA ANGELOU

When faced with sexism or
ageism or lookism or even really
aggressive Buddhism, ask yourself
the following question: "Is this
person in between me and what
I want to do?" If the answer is no,
ignore it and move on. Your energy
is better used doing your work and
outpacing people that way. Then,
when you're in charge, don't hire
the people who were jerky to you.

TINA FEY

.... , 20.........

MON

....

TUE

....

WED

....

THU

....

FRI

....

SAT

....

SUN

....

.... , 20........

MON

....

TUE

....

WED

....

THU

....

FRI

....

SAT

....

SUN

....

Reputation is what others think
about you. What's far more
important is character, because that
is what you think about yourself.

BILLIE JEAN KING

I'm not the next Usain Bolt or
Michael Phelps. I'm the first
Simone Biles.

SIMONE BILES

.... , 20 ....

MON

....

TUE

....

WED

....

THU

....

FRI

....

SAT

....

SUN

....

.... , 20.........

MON

....

TUE

....

WED

....

THU

....

FRI

....

SAT

....

SUN

....

In every position that I've been in, there have been naysayers who don't believe I'm qualified or who don't believe I can do the work. And I feel a special responsibility to prove them wrong.

SONIA SOTOMAYOR

I am not free while any woman is
unfree, even when her shackles are
very different from my own.

AUDRE LORDE

.... , 20.........

MON

....

TUE

....

WED

....

THU

....

FRI

....

SAT

....

SUN

....

.... , 20.........

MON

....

TUE

....

WED

....

THU

....

FRI

....

SAT

....

SUN

....

It's time to order your

the
FEMINIST
agenda

undated agenda

Take this form to your book or stationery dealer, or mail to:

UNIVERSE PUBLISHING

300 Park Avenue South

New York, NY 10010

Included is my check / money order for *The Feminist Agenda*
(please make check payable to Universe Publishing):

_____ copies @ $15.99 each   _____

Postage/handling (Continental U.S. only): Add shipping zone rate   _____
(Zone rates: East $9.00; Midwest $10.00; West $11.00)
For shipping outside the Continental U.S., call 1–800–52-BOOKS for freight quote.

For multiple copies, add $1.00 per copy   _____

Subtotal   _____

New York State residents add 8.875% sales tax   _____
(on subtotal including shipping)

Total amount of check/money order enclosed   _____

Credit Card: _____ Amex _____ Disc _____ MC _____Visa
Account Number _____
Exp. Date _____ Card Verification Code (3 or 4 digits) _____
Signature _____

Name _____
Address _____
City_____ State _____ Zip _____
Phone★ _____ Date _____
★Required for all credit card orders.

Please visit our website, www.rizzoliusa.com,
to download your copy of the illustrated calendar catalog.

.... , 20.........

MON

....

TUE

....

WED

....

THU

....

FRI

....

SAT

....

SUN

....

.... , 20.........

MON

....

TUE

....

WED

....

THU

....

FRI

....

SAT

....

SUN

....

I always did something I was a little not ready to do. I think that's how you grow. When there's that moment of "Wow, I'm not really sure I can do this," and you push through those moments, that's when you have a breakthrough.

MARISSA MAYER

You've gotta do things that make you happy. As women, we tend to give away a lot. We take care of a lot of people, and we can't forget to take care of ourselves.

JENNIFER LOPEZ

.... , 20 ....

MON

....

TUE

....

WED

....

THU

....

FRI

....

SAT

....

SUN

....

.... , 20........

MON

....

TUE

....

WED

....

THU

....

FRI

....

SAT

....

SUN

....

Dreams are lovely. But they are just dreams. Fleeting, ephemeral, pretty. But dreams do not come true just because you dream them. It's hard work that makes things happen. It's hard work that creates change.

SHONDA RHIMES

There never will be complete equality until women themselves help to make laws and elect lawmakers.

SUSAN B. ANTHONY

.... , 20 ....

MON

....

TUE

....

WED

....

THU

....

FRI

....

SAT

....

SUN

....

.... , 20.........

MON

....

TUE

....

WED

....

THU

....

FRI

....

SAT

....

SUN

....

If you've got it, flaunt it. And if you don't got it? Flaunt it. 'Cause what are we even doing here if we're not flaunting it?

MINDY KALING

I love having every right to be
as outspoken as I am, as any man
would be.

CHRISSY TEIGEN

.... , 20........

MON

....

TUE

....

WED

....

THU

....

FRI

....

SAT

....

SUN

....

.... , 20........

MON

....

TUE

....

WED

....

THU

....

FRI

....

SAT

....

SUN

....

If you obey all the rules, you miss all the fun.

KATHARINE HEPBURN

I am tired of living in a world
where women are mostly referred
to as a man's past, present, or future
property/possession. I . . . do not.
belong. to anyone. but myself. and
neither do you.

ARIANA GRANDE

.... , 20.........

MON

....

TUE

....

WED

....

THU

....

FRI

....

SAT

....

SUN

....

......................., 20.........

MON

....

TUE

....

WED

....

THU

....

FRI

....

SAT

....

SUN

....

Never think you can't do
anything because you're a woman.
Everything is open to you as a girl.
The future is yours.

CHRISTIANE AMANPOUR

Life is not easy for any of us.
But what of that? We must have
perseverance and, above all,
confidence in ourselves. We must
believe that we are gifted for
something, and that this thing, at
whatever cost, must be attained.

MARIE CURIE

.... , 20 ....

MON

....

TUE

....

WED

....

THU

....

FRI

....

SAT

....

SUN

....

.... , 20 ....

MON

....

TUE

....

WED

....

THU

....

FRI

....

SAT

....

SUN

....

Feminism isn't about making
women stronger. Women are already
strong. It's about changing the way
the world perceives that strength.

G. D ANDERSON

I am an example of what is possible
when girls from the very beginning
of their lives are loved and
nurtured by people around them.
I was surrounded by extraordinary
women in my life who taught me
about quiet strength and dignity.

MICHELLE OBAMA

.... , 20........

MON

....

TUE

....

WED

....

THU

....

FRI

....

SAT

....

SUN

....

Vacation	The Future is Female	Doctor	Date Night	Birthday	Diversity. Equality. Unity.
Fight Misogyny	Rise by lifting others	Vacation	Normalize Equality	Hear me roar!	GIRLS DO IT BETTER
RIOT NOT DIET	To-do	#Girlboss	Rise by lifting others	Anniversary	GIRL POWER!
GIRLS DO IT BETTER	Appointment	HERstory	Dentist	Topple the patriarchy	The Future is Female
Date Night	RULE THE WORLD	GIRL POWER!	Appointment	Fight Misogyny	Doctor
Dentist	PERSIST	My Body. My Choice.	To-do	SUPPORT WOMEN	Diversity. Equality. Unity.
Topple the patriarchy	Anniversary	Hear me roar!	Birthday	HERstory	Normalize Equality
#Girlboss	RULE THE WORLD	RIOT NOT DIET	My Body. My Choice.	PERSIST	SUPPORT WOMEN